REFINERY

GEORGIA
PEARLE
FOSTER

Foster Literary

for Jenkins III, my Captain,

and for my cousin, Shannon,

and for all the Babygirls,
whether or not they were girls

CONTENTS

III

IV

REFINERY

The Grown Gorgon Speaks

He surged through the temple before touch
knew my touch, bowed me beneath his gray
green leagues. My want, not my want? No

one asked.
Bad myth: that hair was ever my main glory,
my pronged pulse to the sea, hauling him in,

or that the jealous goddess caught me
in an eeled shriek, turned my head a soft-
bellied nest. But, you say, I must've prayed

to maul each gaze with a hiss? No. Though
I sometimes still see gods dripping from every
oak, gods in every mushroom, gods in all

the lichens extending their fat shelves—
I sometimes fear I'll see those gods in you.
Now I sit in the cemetery, alone

with their stones. They tried
to make their shields from me.
They tried to split me

into something they could ride:
either feathered, angelic, white with graceful
haunches, or brute, hulk- shouldered and saddled.

3

                    And you? When I look at you,

what will you do? Will your throat cinch?
Will you sprout into stone and erode?
Or can you see me truly, finally:

The god was a mere man. I was only
a Babygirl. No monsters ever
made a monster of me.

I

Before the Wreck

Tempting, to think of my beginning with Momma
as *her beginning*, nights she walked the tracks, nights she ran
the train signals wearing my father's jeans, unzipped,
button extended with a hair tie through the loop.

So much of my life I've wanted to make a mother
of her, reduce her to a pair of arms made to hold me
and the temporary belly swell that brought me wailing
through her. Should she who directed the conductors

through the night shift too be held accountable
for every cargo line and passenger train, every curve
in the rail, the crossties and spikes—I dare you try
to harrow her there. Blink twice, and she'll be off,

molted out of those steel-toed boots to become
a platinum wisp, her mind struck to outpace us all.

Watching Wrestling with My Captain

Praise to the working man, the broad, burnt-amber chested man,
the body's slap on the taut rails, those built bodies slicked with baby oil

sheen and bravado, fists arced to an almost-kiss, never touching,
only flexing. This, my Captain's religion: men who held belly-to-back

on the smallish and grainy bow-fronted TV set that I fought with him
to change, to change

        to cartoons where I could find a golden-crowned
ferocity on her own white horse,
        a bright rainbow girl bringing color back
to earth, again, on her own white horse.

Momma Says

Your father was so dyslexic,
he was done by ninth grade,
had to memorize the whole test

to get his captain's license.
I'm telling you, the whole fucking test.
He wanted so badly for his Babygirl

to read. Did I tell you we got arrested
on our first date? I was driving,
he was so drunk he kept grabbing

at my wheel, tickling me from the shotgun
seat. I try to remember Momma
as anything but the red-lipped

bad bitch who baffles me, her
nails filed sharp to snare,
the polaroids I found tucked

in the Bible's front: her bikini
white and blinding, sprawled
on the hood of some American build,

some steel. I try to imagine her
hitched to any man without
a shotgun held first, and yet

how can I not recall her ironing
our skirts for church? And when I,
first of her shotgun babies,

had grown enough to ask her
But what did you really want?
Her pause held long, and then:

Well, I don't think I knew much
what I should want. I thought
I wanted family, wanted you.

Memorial: A Small Service

Here's the Gulf where he chartered the wealthy,
fortunate voyeurs to the deep. They clinked
their grins, leaned in to the rails, sucked

our salt air. Sunset in the backdrop, sky gone
gold and apricot, a bounty they believed
had been made in their names.

I was four years old, and didn't drown.
I'd worn the yellow bikini he bought,
all appliquéd fish and cerulean glimmer.

Captain pulled me from the undertow,
cradled like a trophy mackerel.
His mustache turned a skyward smile.

He warned against jellyfish
that might grab hold, raise welts.

Here's the Gulf where he chartered crews
back and forth to the rigs.

Make sure, he said, *make sure*
baby's got something in her basket

Easter morning, and he left
for the docks at Grand Isle.

Men working the rigs should've been
background checked (State law).

Should've been a third man on deck
(to witness, make peace, or diffuse).

Here's where the deckhand
scaled the redfish, knife scraping a setting sky,
clear, no cover, lapping calm for the barnacles.

He always got something for me to do. Won't let me watch
TV like I should. Always got me at these fish, doing his bait,
cutting his snapper, frying em up, and then he complains.
Show off. The scales fell and cracked beneath his bare feet.

That knife brought Captain's blood to the last
crest and ebb. Stab to the chest, stab
to the chest, stab to the neck
till his livelihood let out
on the dock.

Night settled at the horizons
like oil, sheen and hushed.
Fish pecked the surface, sending out
concentric rings in the shallows.

His hard-won health killed him faster,
arteries unclogged, built muscles surging,
blood strong-going out the wounds.

Shame his flesh couldn't send word
back to heart: slow down, slow down,
you dumb fucking muscle.

The ascendant darkened at the margins.
Cumulocirrus striped our nights like lit sand.
Red tide in the boat's engine housing,

traces all over the deck, the seafoam tinged,
ribboning orange at the shoreline.
It will take years to get a death certificate.

Years I will lay head to pillow
and all my neck's nerves will remember
his neck, punctured, pulled apart,
and each August, mid-August,

the Perseids shower from the radiant—
the sky set to burst, while the cirrus

swirl as vespers and swallow stars
like plums with their horrible hope.

From the Deckhand's Confession:

I told him I wasn't doing nothing, I refused.
He says, long's I'm your captain you'll do
how I say you do.

We started in the galley kitchen, engines
was off. I was upstairs in the wheel house
and he called me from the bunk.

Knife got a wooden handle, bout five inches
with a single edge. I grabbed it, he clawed me
at the shoulders.

That's when I started jigging him with it.
Then he went to biting me. I seen his body
float a while, then after I didn't see.

I went to collect our shorts and tennies,
sent them overboard with a ten pound moll.
Blood rolled down the hall to bunk at our beds.

He captained out to the deep
to dump him, tied off to the West Delta platform,
tried to pully his body overboard.

Instead roped his dead head off—
Daddy's body deposited
into our Gulf, into my bank account,

his skull slow drifting
toward an ocean floor.

Now August jellies build their swarms
and pulse at the platform's base: *Aurelia aurita,*
please promise to drown out the stars.

Memorial wreaths: the floral foam cut
into anchor, life preserver, pierced

with lily of the valley, roses, I wanted
azaleas but they're not florist's flowers.

Still we pick each stem into place.
What's left past story, elegy?

A crucifix in filigree?
A gold sailfish on a fine chain.

After Our Captain's Passing

Momma dragged her grief-sacked ass
downtown to the CSX station.
They made me come to work, she said,

no one else who was qualified
to do the operator's job had had enough sleep.
I went into the control room. Shut the door.

Told everyone to go to hell, and I sat there,
cutting the lights off and on, off and on,
telling the trains where to go.

In the Courtroom Pews

Momma sat so close to the evidence box
she could smell the blood and brine
on the rope, and on the black reeboks

that the deckhand weighted and sank
when he was docked. Our Captain gone,
I'd grow with my own evidence box:

the wooden anchor shellacked with baby
conchs, the three tiger cowries
painted with ghosts, the cyclist medals,

the gold-glinting sailfish I'd wear
across my clavicle, the dreams
that one day he could come water-walking

out of the Gulf, hair matted with sargassum,
ready to raise me, able to clear the sand
from all our throats.

At the Wrongful Death Settlement

The maritime insurance man smiles.
What's behind those clean teeth?
Something clenched, not porous,
a cavern where the gulf-spray collects

and sobs down the limestone.
Say an eye is worth some bookshelves.
How many? Depends how you treat
your pennies. Say a nostril each

to the memorial wreaths, the bridge
of a nose for the glasses she'll need,
a tooth to each set of clothes she'll
outgrow

                      a torso to the esteemed
Mister, attorney at sea, for the trouble—
a handful of toes to Momma, for the grief.

Not that she was too hungry,

but hungry.   Momma knew the exchange
for a well-turned   eyelash, a well-pitched
sob.   Say she's like the sea sparkle
algae—not that they mean   to feed on spilt oil,

or bloom with the river runoff   sloughed
from the heartland farms,   gathered in tributary
then dumped   at the silt mouth of the Gulf,
but still,   give them silt,   and algae will eat
the water clearer,   will open up   the dead
       zones in the Gulf.   Say Babygirl grows

like jellyfish,   like a sea nettle bloom,
specifically,   say one day she'll have a medusa cap
of tendrils,   will flourish   in the space
that algae makes—   hypoxia can strangle
out the fish,   but nettles don't need
      so much oxygen,   need mostly
         the open deep.

II

At the Vanity

Sea sparkle algae lights at the touch
to make beautiful, attracting predators
to eat its predators.

Momma draws a harness round her eyes,
deep blue, deeper, taps her brushes:
powder, lowlight, cheekbones, highlight.

I help zip the back of her gown,
all sequins and aqua glimmer.
Her voice lilts gravel to acetone swoon.

Vanilla, gardenia, cool cool water,
her hair a gasp in platinum, set to light
whole shores, a ghost tide at dusk.

Ghosts in the Confederate House

Down the long cockleshell drive
    smattered with red-seeded cones
        from the magnolia tree,
            up the porch where the old man

hung himself, past the standard
    columns in Corinthian white,
        this, our rented home
            where supposed confederate soldiers

still thrummed through the halls
    most nights, yammering about
        their lost limbs, lost lives,
            lost children and lost wives.

I never heard nor saw them,
    but figured we'd found some portal
        to the damned hinterlands, or hoped
            anyhow, and kept my ears primed

to catch my Captain in the corridors.
    Once, my cousin claimed
        she followed him up the midnight stairs
            then watched him fade into air. Once,

my cousin claimed she had a vision
    of a bad man being bad with me
        and woke Momma in the witching
            hour to tell, but Momma pulled a seat

in the kitchen to put her in, took a pile
of slim round brushes, wrapped and knotted
my cousin's baby-blonde hair, all the while singing
child, fool child, you didn't see a thing.

Some Fairy Tale

At the train yard, Momma'd gone cocaine slim,
rail thin. Danny was a freight inspector, his gaze primed

to splice hard ores back together, a dimpled charmer
with a hint of blue suede in his eyes, smooth

like his well-landed parents, his mayor father,
his mother in her wide-brimmed church hat.

Soon, they'd brought me a brother, then a new home
made in each other, two perfect phantoms descending

our staircase: Momma in her cerulean sequins and tulle,
her neck wrung in platinum and pearls, Danny in his tux

and white bowtie, expert in gentility, buttoned up,
the couple dashing together on their way to the ball.

Refinery
Down by the Bay

After school we'd set our oxfords on the pier,
socks stuffed under their tongues, and I'd strip
off my plaid pinafore, down to my gym shorts
and blouse. Brother'd shed his slacks. We'd bolt
hand in hand over the boat launch into the bay
and the brine, steeping with the moon jellyfish.
We'd pitch and dodge, shrieking glee. Pitch:
to throw outward. Pitch: a substance, amber
black and hyper viscous, which can shape
a solid polish on mirrors, on lenses for spectacles.
As children, wading, we'd pull up dark toefuls
of crude, smear the shining globs in eachother's
hair, let our white blouses tinge, earth like.
Good we left our glasses with our shoes.

Changing Shifts

When Danny got switched to third
and Momma got stuck with the split-shift,

she'd tuck me into her passenger seat
before dawn could break over the bay,

and some mornings there'd be oatmeal
in the ladies' lounge, windows where

the gulls would gather and sift pebbles
in the train yard searching out a treat.

Others, I'd be stolen away to the Sunset
Limited coach car, where I could study

the velvety seats while he did what he'd do
to me—either way, I'd be in my elementary

plaid pinafore by day, in the school line
on time, ready to read and genuflect sweetly.

Babygirl Prayed Alone in the Church

Recesses, I'd steal away to the pews and
make my demands of the Virgin:

Can a sin be forgiven?
       Asking for me, the sin.

The Boiling Pot

I carved play stories
in the sand with my stick,

barefoot, the bottoms
of my feet grey-orange

with earth. I crouched
in the mound, and the ants rose,

beady red bodies swarming
a faint tickle over my skin.

They synchronized under
my canopy of gingham,

under my matching lilac
bloomers, where not even

Momma's peach-tree
switch sung its welts,

where only Danny's unbuckled
belts and workman's hands

and the soft sting and sting
of his tongue would go.

Once the bites had raised
their hard, small bumps,

Momma filled her stockpot
to the brim, boiled it. Poured

a steady massacre over
the mound.

Driveway Down a Dirt Road in the Rain

Thanks be to the monsoons when red
slip pooled in the potholes, when Brother

and me got together in our suits. Sharks
on his, mine a yellow bikini with angelfish.

We'd plop ourselves in the biggest crater,
slippery thick water high on our chests.

Thanks be to dirty. Thanks be to fresh
crepe myrtle overhead. Thanks be to Brother,

who'll grow into the man who's always
and ever good to me. Thanks be to a bawling

sky, to dust pummeled into clots of mud
and sand. Thanks be to slime and scouring.

Danny Tells Me

Babygirl, did you know when I
was in my teens, Grandaddy was mayor

of this town? And oh was I
          a hellion. They couldn't do a thing

to keep me on track. Even so, I was Most Popular,
Star Quarterback, they'd've never

made it to State without me.
          One night about three a.m.,

I'd been throwing quaaludes on top
          of mescaline, and swerving,

when I saw that blue car start
          to creep off the median.

Old boy followed me all the way
          up the driveway, lights-a-spinning,

and I told him he'd better not
          wake my daddy or he'd have

Hell to pay with the Mayor.
I've never seen a cop turn to a whisper

and cut off his flashers so fast. He slow rolled
out and off our street, just like that.

Nothing Stopping Their Plenty

Danny said *Grandmother's*
gonna get them bluegum
coloreds off our street.

Brown recluse
in the berry patch
got her right on the ribs.

Clean up their bald, tired
yard, the scattered toys.
Gonna buy that house

outright, she is, make right.
Grandmother pulled up
her poplin blouse to show skin,

the emanating rot.
Went on to bake
her cobbler anyhow.

Babygirl stabbed up
the berries, folded
them into buttercrust,

couldn't eat. Stab, fold,
stab, till the plate turned
pulp and bruise.

Dominion in the Garden

Grandmother left her sweet dogwood
    untouched, his bark soft and tan,
smooth, that handsome tree she dropped
    into the soil, a seasoned bride.

But the myrtle's branches she cut to shy
    nubs, their fawn-like stalks bound
at the base. Brother and I pried
    scuppernongs off vines all afternoon.

Tongued the mucous-thick fruit
    from its hull, spit and lazed
in the fresh, shorn dew.
    Then, by my ankle bone,

the grasshopper, mottled and marked,
    vigilant in design (as Grandmother said
all good seeds are). She swiped the grass,
    cracked her open, twisted the head

off her ochre abdomen to discard it,
    legs still bounding, trailing eggs.
Grandmother thought she was culling
    undesirables from her bed.

Then I scraped up the guts,
        tucking them three inches down
in the packed ground. Mounted
        velvetleaf flags at the nape

of the mound. The myrtle will send out
        new shoots in spite, will keep fuchsia
fuming beneath her green. *Dear God*
        we ain't meant to stay in her way, Amen.

Freedom Tour

One Sunday, Danny loaded me
in his old white Chevy to drive me
across the Causeway to Africatown,

across the train tracks and past
the paper mill's sulfur stink, he meant
to show me what it means to get Free.

Grandmother and Granddaddy's
family used to own people like these,
and don't let nobody tell you

how bad things used to be. Back
in those days, people knew who
was feeding them, and those slaves?

Why, they could dance and play
on the whole wide plantation
after a day's work was done. Now

look at them. I looked across the street,
through the rusted chain links,
to a brown girl in bare feet carving

play-stories in the dirt with her stick.
I looked at her. She looked at me.
And my hatred for him burst

into bloom, and its perfume enclasped
us in the truck—big, bigger than
Sunday dinner, bigger than all magnolias.

Then the Plenty Stopped Caught in Her Throat

Cobbler, butterbeans, honey ham,
pigs' feet, redeye gravy, jello cakes,
Grandpa grinned sick as we dolloped

our plates: *Careful. That'll make ya pretty.*
Starving, then the glut and purge,
grew in my gut come puberty.

Body said, I know who's feeding me.
I'll stay hungry till the bones
show through like slats.

III

Playing Victim

I perched on the bathroom sink to apply a drama
of plum eyeshadow to my cheekbone's crest, pinched

my lips to wrench out more swollenness. His aftermath.
I was his old-enough-to-know-better darling, who'd forgot

to wait at his stair top and flourish his fresh tea.
He'd never hurt me where Momma could see, so

I'd outline the bruise till color broke through my stubborn
capillaries, their flexible walls: a show to give Momma at last.

Consider the Monster

You want to believe you'd know
him from regular, but you chose him
Most Popular, teeth all aglimmer
same year he raped his kid sister.

I've got the yearbook proof.
You want to pitchfork
against my Momma's taste
in men? You made his daddy mayor
time and again.

Look at your ownselves. Look in.
You want to know my loving him,
my making him Daddy of mine,
puts the fact of the doorframe
on me, takes away my choke and suffocate.
How quaint.

         When the devil said dance,
we danced. When the devil said smile,
we smiled. When the devil's a man
upstanding, it takes newsprint to spin him
long-sentence-in-prison ugly.

Daphne, Alabama, 1999

Had my snatch of rope in the car trunk,
thought to splay him out on the freight
tracks. I wanted him branded above
his sob-sorry eyes. Then the cicadas sent

their aubade my way, sang: *We'll make Danny*
our dogwood tree, all delicacy, blossoms gone
green at the center. We'll chew slits along his
branches, make him ground for a new brood.

Let us send our nymphs to hatch, drop and dig
through the soil to his roots and sip. Too many
years we sucked his bad sap, years we waited
to ascend as swarm, all sharp wings and song.

Night Drive

One Sunday, after sunset, I demanded
        Danny take my passenger seat,

light me one of his Marlboro Reds.
        He did. *And where are we going?*

he said, but I'd already shut silent
        as an underwater swarm.

Sixteen, I sped the neighborhood streets
        till he turned sick. I wanted him

pleading, waiting the length
        for my rage to come clean,

churning on my axis of need:
        "Danny, I wrote it all down,

what you've been doing to me. You
        and Momma will emancipate me.

You are going to let me get free."

At the Sheriff's Station

You sure, young lady? That's not
> *how it sounded to me. He said*
>> *you were older, wanted it. He said*

you couldn't get enough of it.
> *I bet your Momma wouldn't let*
>> *him have enough of it, I bet*

a good looking guy like that
> *must've been hungry, trapped.*
>> *I bet he couldn't help it. I bet*

you knew you could use your
> *ways to get what you wanted from this.*
>> *Think you'll get what you wanted from this?*

Danny

Collapsed one day on the prison
concrete, a clotted block in his brain.

The obituary listed survivors;
"survived by" did not include me.

*I'd been praying that night for his
peace*, Momma called to say,
Babygirl, I'd been praying for peace.

My Enemy is Dead; A Man Divine as Myself is Dead

Alone, I brought my baby's breath
bouquets to the feet of your trinity:

Grandmother's headstone in the center,
Grandaddy's at left, Danny's at right,

simple and gray as doves. Whose justice
is ever just enough? I yanked fistfuls

of grass from your graves. It feels nearly
yesterday that I saw you in cuffs, escorted

away, can still hear you mouthing
as you silently say, I'm sorry, Babygirl.

So sorry. I know, I say aloud to the cemetery
today. Lone survivor among survivors,

I didn't show. I wouldn't bend
to touch your white face in the coffin.

Momma Tries to Die

And I don't know how to look on her
with anything but fury, her in her sad mute

hospital gown, so I settle my knuckles
on her wax forehead, imagine I can pull

the long-gone ballgowns from behind
her eyelids, peel the long-lost sequins

from her nipples, release the angels
from her ears. On my way to this infirmary,

I stole the grape-leaf earrings off her
jewelry tree. Mother, thanks be to your

impossibility, to your long sobs after my
bedtime, to the faltering notes you sang

me all the way to school. To your raucousness,
your lust, even your angel dust. Here

among the machines, you tell me I'm haloed.
You tell me I'm your own mother, reborn, or

the white witch, the healer in my hands.
Now isn't the time to tell you how

limited I am. I can barely bear you, can't
put your mind back in place. I only

take my thumb and trace the stitches
in your face. Drugged and dizzy, you fell

and fell on your busted vase, and here we are
laughing (you saying, Just call me Grace.)

And oh mother of course you are grace—
we're caught in so many unearned moments,

like when I slake the voice you gave me
out my throat and sling it through

the hospital halls. Mother, oh whatever,
of course we may stay shattered, still singing.

IV

He Never Split My Skin

Instead, his hangdog
sob nested and bred

in me, hymen stretched
so quietly it could've

been myth. Now,
when I love, I want

it hard as can get,
petrified, someone

to wrench in and core
his soft violence out.

First Crush

Down Earlville Road the orange dust
kicks up with every passing pickup truck,
and I watch my first crush, dusk settling
on his shoulder blades, sweat damping
the hair my fingers once tangled.

I watch him thrust the mower
through thick grass, watch it spit
out behind him. Mostly it's his shoulders
I watch, wrought and gristled.
I can't touch them now.

One time his sisters came
to Momma's house on Creekside Drive.
City girl, they called me,
girl who can't axe chickens,
who don't have to share her bed.
They never talked as freely once they'd seen
the three flights of stairs in our suburban split-level.

They must have brought home stories
(Momma's rosebud china
inside our lit oak hutch)
because here I am stooping
by his Meemaw's rusted frigidaire,

ice sweating out the glass
I poured him, and I can't pull
even his gaze toward mine.

In My Girlfriend's Dorm Room

I press my ear in the curve
of her breast, hook my knees
into the angle of her knees.

My thigh throbbed: I'd driven
the straight edge across my skin,
carved my body into being mine.

I'd tried to make the lie of my life
visible. The girl I was didn't know
any other way. Her hands pressed

cool along my skin's scabbed text.
Her arms, the first place I'd learn
to hold delicate skin—her skin, my own.

Somewhere outside her window, past
the dormitory's square of grass, past
the marbled saints and saltless fish

on Fridays, we heard the train,
the low moan of someone else's
cargo shunting through the pines.

Underbelly

Late night. Bonfire swells near the fish pond,
and the boys are just getting going good.
I've got my feet against the flames, feel the soles

of my black maryjanes melting into themselves.
Can't move, Satan's dancing his white-glow face
around the climbing heat. They're drunk,

throwing tires into the fire and Gabriel shouts,
Hey! That smells just like hot tar burnin! while I turn
the eyes that love you up toward

specks gleaming in the dark, and Amazing Grace
sends up its bagpipe notes in the distance. But now
the tailgate's dropped on their old Ford,

someone's started a stereo, someone's shouting
Freebird! and the hollering goes up in rounds while
I press the lips that love you inward

to memories of your dark curve of neck,
earlobes, the fingers I sucked long and slow.
The boys are bashing beercans, swaying

singing far as I can figure, there's nothin
quite as worthless as a white girl with a ------
while I fold the hands that love you, prim,

remembering how I kneaded your crown
on down to the small of your back.
Now Michael's caught a catfish, slippery

silver, mouth puckering gasps in the brisk air.
He glides his knifeblade along the spine.
They're best fried fresh, while the blood's

still pumpin. He rubs the slick underbelly,
slides his thumbnails into the split fish
neck, pulls the skin off slow.

Jubilee City
Daphne, Alabama

I can still see us, insurgent shadows
on the bay, summer braying in the atmosphere.

Our clothes loose, ungendered. I was probably
wearing your pants, I'm sure you had on my

black socks. It was the night of the jubilee,
our consecration on the pier in Daphne,

the flounders, the eels, the blue crabs brought
close to shore, not enough oxygen in the water,

this sudden abundance, my ache for you a new
liberty and I don't know how we breathed

submerged in each other's gasping and groping,
my back scraped bare against the concrete slab,

our mouths hopeful, gaping like caught
trout contorting themselves toward home.

Sunset Limited

After the wreck, they drove me down
where the charred cars lay stacked by
the highway's wayside. *Look, girl.*

Seagulls bobbed and plunged at loosed
saltines. Frog calls blistered in the background.
There must have been stretchers brought,

helicopters circling in huntress swarms,
radioed calls to tote the dead away.
The train that pummels off into bayou,

that's all Momma drawn to the bogs,
no mind to her ribs, steel and bowed,
pregnant with passengers. She thinks

she's a gilled fortress. Her iron
shudders and shouts through the pines.
A woman is neither train nor wreck,

but he was the barge in fog that sent
her track akimbo? No. Not barge, not man.
A girl is neither track nor last halt.

II.

I got to drive that train once.

Sat on the conductor's lap.

I guess it was less driving,

more pulling a string to let

the whistle croon long-loud.

He'd pulled on his jumpsuit

that hazed September morning,

when the sky still hung pitch,

to help the bog-drenched,

the drowned, shaken bodies

from the flaming Canot. The train,

later: steel split under the weight

of its own derailment, passengers

all dispersed, the small crook

of bayou still speckled with oil.

Today you called me a train

wreck. Maybe I am more

like the girl I was, sitting

in your conductor's lap,

the view of my own sunset

limited. I have never been a train.

V

Refinery
Jubilee City

My father could not read for pleasure, rather, he read
how sheetrock needed to set square against a new home's
frame, read the lines of 40 lb test and wrestled with reels,
red snapper and mackerel. My father read the trawlers'
tall masts, picked through the bait fish, jellyfish, cuttlefish.
My father knew how to keep what to keep. With his blood
money we bought me books, navy cardigans and pinafores
and some supposed way out, away from the egrets, gone
from undertow and tide and man-o-war shores, no more
mollusks in sand. Father, with you gone, my hands grew
dyslexic, my air kept too filtered, tempered. Forgive me
this refinement. Forgive me how we paid for it.

Refinery
Texas City

In my passenger seat she crosses
her legs, pulls down the sun visor.

Near midnight, and the perseids
send slow artillery across our sky.

We've got a full tank, driving past
the derricks and pump jacks;

the sucker rods bob in the fields
like bored horses. *My uncle died*

in that refinery, she says,
chemical spill. No body left

to bury. Cousins got a settlement.
I say nothing of my Captain,

don't want to heap grief on grief.
She flicks on the visor light

and keeps her gaze to its mirror,
lit, her own eyes on her own lips,

which she daubs a cimmaron red,
her center fingertip bright and greased.

Past the Refinery

Yachts knock in the harbor. Oil tanks
glow full and fat beneath the yellow globes

and smokestacks. Such brights at the refinery,
those sweet lubricants, those rich plumes

that chuff and chug at the sky. Such light
fuel lifted from the residual crude.

Along our shorelines, the spilt sheen's
been sunk, and the sands are sifted white

enough again. Each night I drive home
past the vats. I want to believe I can't help

my mouth, how I'm drawn to cup it round
the inbound pipes. In nightmares I swallow,

swallow, until pitch edges my gums, and silt
slops off my teeth. I don't even pause to breathe.

What Becomes Soil

Here's where we took the canoe out,
pushed off the cross-ties, railroad salvage.

Each floating knot hinted alligators
underwater—was that snout, or bark?

Sometimes cottonmouths curved black
through pine needles, sometimes we swam—

earth, decay, years of dropped leaves
sending up the scent of what becomes soil.

This our first family home, a trailer,
corrugated box the color of nicotine stains,

where it began. Me, Babygirl, six years old,
the shower, him a grown man, thinking himself

a father. My slight body pressed under the sulfur
stink, water pumped deep from the well.

Now it's all ash and charred frames,
yellowhammers nesting into what's left

of roof eaves, their calls pitched
against silence, his remnants

in me like the last twitch of nerves
in a rattlesnake, headless, holding fast.

Refinery
After the Spill

Down in Bayou La Batre, the oysters
sludged in oil, an irritant too slick
to make pearls. Along the coast, thick
yellow boom formed a barrier and crews
set out with skimmers. Still the oysters
choked. I'm sick of writing all the ways
to choke or not to choke. Enough sputtering
metaphor. Enough bays and likenesses
and poor filtering bivalves. We've asked too
much of the oysters, too many times we've said,
here, mollusk, you're stuck in the muck.
What'll you choose to do? Have some grit,
baby, grit— and best make it luminous.

After the Refinery

Some Sundays we used to go crabbing
after Momma got done on the railroad
night shift, she in her cutoffs and crocheted
top, me small in my sandals and in the way.

Now we bring my children to the bay—
we're tourists with our nets but I've not forgot:
tie the twined bait in a sand dollar shape
to the crab baskets' centers, teach

my young one to see the barnacles
working the pilings: look how life blooms
its way into every wrecked pillar,
see how my Momma still pulls

the full baskets up in this town
where the fire station was named for us,
maybe some streets were named for us,
but we've all since changed our names.

Afterword: On Refinement

In the year 1999, there is a girl living in a poem at the end of the world she's known. She doesn't realize it yet, but the nights breathing into her pillow, the nights with no one to hear, are coming to a close. She can't know this, can only feel the nights closing in. She skips full days of high school to thieve away to the city library, where she collects books with titles like *Good Woman*, *The Book of Light*, *A Street in Bronzeville*, and *The Beaneaters* from the sparse shelves, and she piles those books in her lap. She is reading not from curiosity or intellect, but from need. She will need fortified; there will be a trial soon to come, and the things she wrote down in her journal for no one to hear will be entered into evidence. After turning that journal in to the State for prosecution, she will not write for years, and she will barely be able to keep her eyes to a page long enough to read. Still, she sleeps in the library chairs with these books in her lap as if they might ward away what came for her each night before he was taken away, and what will come for her each night after he has been locked away. She keeps these books in her lap and sleeps, as if they could be bricks for her dreams, bricks she might use to build a road and track out of this poem where she lives at the end of the world.

Of course the she is the Babygirl who shows up in *Refinery*. Of course Babygirl is me, and *Refinery* is a memoir-in-poems. In a way, I suppose the moment in which I now live, twenty-some-odd years later, looks something like the road that got built, like some supposed way out.

One of the challenges of writing this book has been how to write the story that is particularly mine while also paying homage to those poets and people who left the light on the path for me, whether or not the light they shone was meant for me specifically. Those books were on the shelf of my library, no doubt, because of the proximity of my hometown to Africatown.

Back when I was Babygirl, we lived less than twenty miles from Plateau, Alabama, where Zora Neale Hurston traveled to interview Kossola "Cudjo" Lewis for the book that would become Barracoon. Back home, nearly nobody I knew called Plateau "Plateau"—I have always known it as Africatown.

Lewis was one of the founders of Africatown, the last living survivor of the Clotilda, which was the last known slave ship to come to the United States, illegally, decades after the slave trade had been abolished. After unloading over one hundred people bought from Dahomey and forced through the Middle Passage, the Clotilda sailed into Bayou Canot, put down anchor, and the men in charge of the ordeal set the ship on fire to destroy the evidence. After the Civil War brought emancipation a few years later, Lewis and several men and women who had been enslaved bought a parcel of land from the man who had bought them. This land would be the beginning of Africatown.

Bayou Canot is also the site of the Sunset Limited wreck, the worst train wreck in Amtrak history. In the middle of a September night in 1993, a tug boat knocked into a low bridge and knocked the train's track off-kilter. When the Sunset Limited passenger train attempted the bridge later that night, it was tracked instead into the bayou, where it submerged and burst into fire, killing forty-seven people.

Back when I was Babygirl, my step-father, Danny, and my mother were both Railroaders, as they called themselves, and Danny was working the night shift for CSX Transportation when the Sunset Limited plunged into the Bayou Canot. Because Danny was a union man, and at the time on the clock for CSX (though he regularly did side shifts for Amtrak to earn extra, cleaning the passenger trains in the early dawn), my mother tells me he wouldn't transgress the union rules to assist the men pulling surviving passengers from the Canot. Instead, she tells me, he kept working—tortured, she tells me, at the screams he could hear across the night, coming from the site of the wreck.

I remember the date of the wreck particularly because it was September 22: my dead father's birthday. I had not known it was my father's birthday until that very morning when my mother stopped me at the door to notice I'd donned a locket with his photo inside. Some part of you knew, she told me, the part of you that chose that locket today, that part of you knew.

After the Sunset Limited had been recovered from the bayou and brought to railroad-owned property just at the base of the then-new Africatown Bridge, Danny took me to survey the wreckage. I was eleven at the time. Danny was keen on history and keen to ensure I learned from these moments. To him, there was something to the looking that explained ourselves to us, somehow. Mostly I think he was trying to set me in touch with my own vulnerability, reinscribe his place as supposed protector. In the looking, though, mostly what I saw was a reiteration of death by human error, human avarice, human greed. In thinking all those people lost to the bayou, I thought of my real father, lost to the Gulf. In thinking about the Clotilda sunk in the bayou, in service to the production of cotton, I thought my father's body sunk in the Gulf, in service to the production of oil. This was my child's sense drawing equations, of course—I don't mean to suggest that these three moments in history are at all on scale with each other. They are not. The Sunset Limited poem in Refinery is an attempt at teasing out the moments where our language draws unfair correlations. I tried in some drafts to add the Clotilda layer to that poem, but my skill fell short.

Danny was also keen to drive me through places that felt forbidden to white traffic, places white people would nearly never go. One of these places was Africatown, Plateau, then on up through Pritchard, until we'd hit the interstate that runs to Montgomery on the other side.

On these trips, he'd warn me about the people who lived in Africatown, claiming that they would intentionally wreck their own cars, and ours too, if it might open an avenue to sue us. *You have to watch out for these people. They have a victim mentality. Few things are worse than a victim mentality. They think the world owes them something.* Danny's narration of this human history, of course, did not bear any resemblance to truth. Take for instance Cudjo Lewis's account in Barracoon. He was hit by an L&N train after the company laid tracks through his community, and injured badly enough to disable him. A white lawyer offered to represent him in a lawsuit against the railroad company, and won the case, but then absconded with the small compensation Lewis was awarded.

Later, Lewis's son lost his life to a train on the same tracks.

Not long after the Sunset Limited wreck, Danny drove me in his bright white Chevy truck over that bridge into Africatown. Once we'd hit the streets where the pavement wasn't quite so smooth, where the houses clung together more closely and the people in them kept to their front porches more often than I'd seen in other parts of town, he motioned for me to move closer to him, into the crook of his arm, across the bench seat. I complied. I always complied. *Look* he beckoned me. *This is what happened to the Africans who thought they'd get free.*

I could see the lesson he meant to teach me: if I thought I could get out from beneath him, I'd find poverty lunging for me the likes of which I'd never truly seen, and I should fear that, and the people already living in it, more than I should ever fear what he had in store for me at home.

This is the fear bred in service of white supremacy, and Danny was of course trying to make a white "us" loom larger than any other "we" I might find.

We see this fear reiterated constantly in service of larger political goals. Poor and working class white southerners have some inkling of how much worse it could be when they look to a community like Africatown.

The fatal flaw in Danny's use of this fear against me, back then, was that I knew that it was men like him—and his wealthy family who hoarded their resources, refusing to let black people into their many businesses or any of their many rental properties until the federal government intervened decades past the legal mandate to integrate—who had something to do with this poverty across the color line. And I already knew who he was behind that genteel façade.

Just as he was finishing his stump speech, I saw the girl through the fence, carving words into the dirt with a stick like I'd loved to do when I was younger. I thought of my cousin, Kelli, two years older, just older enough for me to idolize, and the letters she'd been sending me all summer from South Carolina. My cousin wasn't black as the girl on the other side of that fence, but she was blacker than me, a gift from her mother, who was black and Northern, who served in the United States Army, who'd told me never to call her "ma'am" again. It occurred to me that this enemy that Danny tried to make for me was not much of an enemy at all. This so-called enemy was more kin to me than he'd ever be.

I know what white supremacist ideology did to Danny because I lived under the thumb of it: it sunk into all his cells and made him believe, and believe entirely, in his right as a white man to subjugate and use whatever bodies he could, in whichever way he pleased. I wondered for a moment, that day in Africatown, if he'd been able to keep a true slave, one that could never get free, would he have needed to turn to me? That's another question I can't help thinking he meant to wrest from me: the one which might have made me glad to think someone else should be beneath me.

I was not interested, however, in seeing him bring horrors to others in place of me. I did not want anyone else's life to be truncated in place of mine. I wanted the horrors themselves gone. I wanted some new way of being to be born for us all, but I have always been good at wanting the impossible. I would have to start with making some version of my own small life tolerable enough to keep going.

2019: In the final year of my PhD program, my cousin Shannon calls me on the phone, and when I answer she thinks she's misdialed the number. So much education has taken the home out of my voice. She no longer recognizes me. Now I put my prepositions in all the wrong-but-proper places, my vowels and consonants alike have been clipped of their drawl. I sound vaguely New England, mostly middle-America, an educated anywhere. It seems the only place that the home grown sog in my throat shows up anymore is in my poems.

The price of education, of supposed refinement, was the price of my voice. I'm not talking about accents alone. I'm talking about the fact that now I vibrate sound more through the upper tier of my face—nose and cheekbones—than deep in my jaw and throat. I'm talking about diction and tone, the way the throat moves octaves, or handles pitch, the way my mother can't speak two sentences without cursing thrice but I only let that language fly among familiars.

I've nearly left behind, even forgotten, the sort of speech that, if transfixed to a page, immediately sounds false to a reader somehow, contrived, and it sounds contrived because people who talk like that almost never write books about themselves, themselves. They get read, if they get read, always through a more learned filter, or they "get out" and become the filter themselves.

As an undergraduate, the distinction between the home voice in my poems and my newly collegiate speaking voice was brought to my attention abruptly, by a woman who had been involved in organizing a poetry competition in which I was asked to compete.

Just before the competition, I was seated between two judges at a table covered with overwhelming layers of fabric, an unnecessary amount of forks, wine in the glasses and steaks on the plates with fine rosemary sprigs in the potatoes. I could tell I was being too quiet as I listened to the other competitors amble through their conversations quickly, all with an excited pitch that seemed to match roundly. Then came the *Where are you from?* which I always hated answering when New Englanders were asking, for fear of being mistaken for a belle, or worse, for fear of having to explain how not a belle I am to people who couldn't tell a ditch from a debutante. Where are you from? meant I'd have to answer for Alabama some way, and even now I know I'll never have enough answers to answer for Alabama. Still, I told the judge I was from Alabama. Oh, she said, you don't sound at all like you're from the South.

I didn't say clearly you've missed my spotlight in the newspaper recently, because it sure seemed good and Bamatrash to me that my second husband had been carted away on drug charges after a domestic violence call that month, and we'd hit the local papers and the college rag with that mess, and the college judicial board was trying to decide if that warranted kicking me out, too, what with two months to go to graduation. Some things don't wash away with the dean's list or with writing awards, it seemed. And it sure seemed Bamatrash to me that I was now not only someone who grew up "abused," not to mention being the daughter of people who came home with fingernails greased to the quick the color of crude oil, but also a single mother to two kids with two different fathers at the ripe wantonness of twenty-seven. The social worker who'd checked in to make sure my kids weren't being neglected had said, well, women with backgrounds like yours tend to repeat the cycle of violence without knowing it.

Really? I said to the Judge at dinner. Sure seems to me like I'm from the South. Can't say why you're not hearing it.

Later that night, reading my poems onstage, I sure enough sounded like the South, though constrained to the stanzas, fettered, unfriendly. Morose. Slipping into my past on the page brought it back, in that spotlight haze where no faces can be made out and the audience fades into shuffling sounds and breath. On stage, transfixed, I could meander and drawl as I had on the page, and I did.

Days later, someone tangential to the event, who'd been with the judges, caught me walking the campus path past the library. I just thought you should know, she said, then paused, breathed deep, and for a second pinched her lips tight between her teeth before resting her hand on my forearm. *I just thought you should know that there was—talk—some talk—among the judges—that your reading was a bit—performed—it's just that it seemed—you know—you don't talk like that—it seemed a bit—contrived.*

In that moment on the sidewalk by the library, I knew the only acceptable response was gratitude. I nodded, trying to cue that I was serious in my consideration of this criticism. I smiled. I said, Thank you. I hadn't considered that I might be contriving my voice. I said, I appreciate your letting me know.

Ten years in hindsight, it's hard not to be amused that the voice that I was accused of contriving was the voice closest to my own and to my home, that neither the judges nor the well-meaning liaison considered that my voice at the table-clothed dinner was in fact the voice I'd performed for them, honed to match the setting, meant to make my difference invisible as I could muster. The thing that kept closest to their comfort became the thing they read as true.

It was also not lost on me, the first time I heard students stroll across campus using phrases like *to whom was she speaking?*, that many of my affluent white peers had grown up using language that was formally accurate. Not all of us had to choose between "authenticity" and formal credibility in our language.

How do I describe the loss that comes with becoming unrecognizable to my own home? I am the only one in my whole extended family, save one cousin with a bachelor's degree, to have put myself through any degree, much less a PhD, and this transformation began with my father's murder. I would not have gotten the education I did had he not been killed on the job, and had the court system not ruled in favor of my welfare.

A wrongful death suit was filed against the crew boat company and the maritime insurance company after he died. My mother tells me cars started following her, that there were private investigators hired to discredit her character in court and show we were undeserving of compensation. My mother, who'd always been wild and mouthy, became fanatic about keeping appearances.

Only twenty-seven herself at the time, she was learning the hard way what can happen when someone has grounds, any grounds, to judge a person unworthy. She made sure to dress conservatively. She never succeeded in taming her speech, but she shamed herself mercilessly for the way she spoke and admonished me not to take her mouth as any example.

Initially, the lawsuit was in the millions, but the settlement came in at a quarter of a million dollars. The litigating attorney took forty percent. Because my parents had been divorced, the estate was set up in my name alone, to be used for my care alone. It did little to change our standard of living, but it did everything to change my access to knowledge. My mother put nearly all the money into educating me out of our class background: extensive grief counseling in kindergarten, Catholic school all the way, boarding school when I was a sophomore in high school. The last of it would go to tuition bills and group therapy in my early twenties. By the time I transferred to Smith College, the estate was spent, and my enormous private tuition bills were covered by my school's endowment, alumnae donors, and student loans.

I keep trying to reconcile the unsettling that comes with having had some major loss compensated through a financial endowment. Growing up, I did literally think of my father as having been put through the grinder of industry, portioned up and given back to us as a set of goods. Of course I know I'm "luckier" than, say, the inhabitants of Africatown, who have had very little recourse for the ways industrial sprawl in downtown Mobile has cost them their community. Any remunerative justice is hardly worth what was lost, if what was lost was a specific living being's health, livelihood, life. What would any of us trade for our dearest loves? Yet where would I be without the justice that made a different life possible for me?

Because my father couldn't read, the myth of him that my mother shaped for me was a sort of savior in the vein of Christ:

he died so that I could have a different sort of life, albeit a life of the mind as opposed to spiritual salvation.

Babygirl, she'd say, *he wanted so badly for you to read.*

In this way, the loss of my father to the oil industry is inextricable from this education that has grown me away from the people who made me. Hence the Refinery that shows up especially in the final section of the book, and my inability to extract it from guilt, ambivalence, grief.

It has been a challenge not to reduce my father and my mother both to figments of my own grief.

For years I could barely manage to write my mother at all, in part because I couldn't extract myself from my rage at her powerlessness, and because it took years to understand her powerlessness as systemic, ranging far wider than her own human will. In the years following my father's murder, my mother became obsessed with our family's optics, with respectability. Marrying into my stepfather's family, with their Old South, church-going, moneyed gentility, became part of that obsession, and when she found out too late what he'd been doing to me, it created a schism in her brain and in her functioning from which she has never fully recovered. She is legally disabled, but ferocious as ever.

My hope is that the poems that handle my mother also recover some value for her as she truly is—complex and forceful, unbridled, full of will that winds up thwarted but only occasionally diminished. I only wish I were skilled enough to make her appear funny on the page more often, because she is horrifically funny.

In a way, the Memorial sequence is both an elegy for my father himself and more an elegy to the person I could no longer become, with him gone, as well as a gesture to who I would need to become in his absence.

The first piece of the poem was a means of framing my rage at the myths of deservingness that people with good fortune often like to carry, this notion that god/the universe rewards people who are good and doles out just desserts.

Most of the italicized text that's in the murder's voice in the Memorial sequence was lifted from the taped interview conducted by Detective Steve Buras in the Jefferson Parish Sheriff's Office after my father's murderer was arrested, in the process of his being questioned, and most of the specific details in the poem were also lifted from this document, though I shaped what I lifted for rhythm, altered tenses, and arranged it for poetic logic in the poem itself.

The interview itself was thirteen typed pages, which gave me plenty of variations in phrase and a solid sense of the murderer's voice from which to draw a likeness on my own pages. I am still at times discomfited at having taken his voice, and its deep Cajun dialect, and twisting it to my own ends in the poem. Then I remember that he killed my father, while I rearranged a few of his sentences, and given that fact I'm okay with my balance on the scales of justice.

The danger I sensed in writing these poems, because they are so deeply autobiographical, was that they were at risk of dismissal due to their subject matter. Either they'd be undeservingly dismissed and considered diminutive, because, truly, who wants to read poems about a sad little girl being abused? This is not the stuff of serious literature, if you believe so many generations of critics—except of course in the case that we're reading from the vantage point of the sad villain. Then the work is "groundbreaking." Worse, however, was the possibility that I might be leaning on the salaciousness of my life and fail as an artist, because the audience came in support of content as opposed to whatever skill I might bring to the page. I remain ambivalent about the balance of skill and content, generally, and I remain unconvinced that the two exclude each other by anything other than happenstance. The subjects on which one may write horribly have no bounds, and any reader may close any book they please for any reason they please.

Meanwhile, how can we be anything but ambivalent when we live in a world in which human lives are sacrificed regularly at the altar of other people's desires? Sure, there's Danny, and his family, as they appear in the book, as the obvious examples, and there's no love I know more intimately than ambivalent love, the sort of love that injures and then soothes, tightening the bond with each successive injury and each soothing that follows, but tragedy—especially in our hyper-connected post-internet reality— is so common, it's become banal.

I nonetheless hope that Refinery shows survivorship as something that can inhabit greater complexity than current and prominent thinking about trauma has allowed. I mean for the book to ask us to consider what happens next once we've loosed ourselves from the patriarchs in their varying degrees of violence and benevolence. What do we choose to become, then? How do we get to a place where more of us actually can choose lives that don't leave us or anyone else hobbled by circumstance? How do we keep showing up in spite of the onslaughts in our days?

I hope that the book opens up more possibilities than it forecloses. I hope it brings its readers into a different understanding of what it means to love, the complicated nature of community and constraint. I do hope it manages to redeem, somehow, someway. I think we're all in need of a different sort of redemption in the days to come, a way out from under the old modes of dominion.

NOTES

The italicized text in "Memorial: A Small Service" was taken from the September 18, 1986 transcript of a taped statement in which Detective Steve Buras interviewed Joseph Paul Vinet, a white male, in reference to the homicide of Jenkins Leslie Nelson III, for which Vinet was later convicted. Creative liberties were taken in the ordering of the text.

The italicized text in "After Our Captain's Passing" was taken from an interview of Lorie Nelson Ellis in September 2015.

The final lines of "Freedom Tour" are an allusion to Gwendolyn Brooks, "A Bronzeville Mother Loiters in Mississippi. Meanwhile, a Mississippi Mother Burns Bacon."

"My Enemy is Dead; A Man Divine as Myself is Dead" is titled from lines in Walt Whitman's "Reconciliation," and the final lines of the poem are also an allusion to the aforementioned poem.

"First Crush" is for Lil' Allen, whose grandmother Rita lived down Earlville Rd.

"In My Girlfriend's Dorm Room" is for Mary Peterson Burts.

"Underbelly" is for Abdul Aziz.

"Jubilee City" is for Jason Albright.

All of the Captain/Daddy poems in the book are for Jenkins Leslie Nelson III.

ACKNOWLEDGMENTS

Grateful acknowledgement to Simmons Buntin and Derek Sheffield at Terrain.org, as well as the editors at Women's Studies Quarterly and Naugatuck River Review, and the now-defunct modmobile.com, in which these poems first appeared, sometimes in earlier versions.

Immense gratitude as well to The Nelson Family, The Ellis Family, Kathleen Hirsch, Elizabet Elliott, Mary Peterson Burts, Pam Lacey, Smith College, Erika Lacquer, Susan Van Dyne, Annie Boutelle, Ellen Doré Watson, Nikky Finney, Hilton Als, Kimberly Rogers, C. Grace Chang, Hannah Wren Won, Katherin Hudkins, Renate Robertson, Jennifer Williams, Lesley University, Teresa Cader, Thomas Sayers Ellis, Cate Marvin, Erin Belieu, Enzo Silon Surin, Mary Hutchins Harris, Lisa Pegram, Mary Benson, Jennifer Fitzgerald, University of Houston, Gulf Coast: A Journal of Literature and Fine Arts, J. Kastely, Kevin Prufer, Martha Serpas, Maria Gonzales, Amanda Ellis, Misty Matin, Miah Arnold, Raj Mankad, Inprint Houston, Yerra Sugarman, Luisa Muradyan, Michele Nereim, Kate Highfill, Jeffrey R. Villines, Christopher Brean Murray, Niki Herd, William Burns, JP Gritton, Aliah Lavonne Tigh, Erika Jo Brown, Dino Piacentini, Josephine Mitchell, Rachel Fairbank, Brenden & Sarah & Elizabeth Oliva, Joshua Dewain Foster, Phyrex Hasten Pearle, and Aurelius Asriel Pearle